Contents

KT-468-462

Good manners

People with good manners know
how to behave in different places.

If you have good manners, people will enjoy taking you out.

Show people your manners

Don't be rude when you speak to people.

Say "please" and "thank you" when you ask for something.

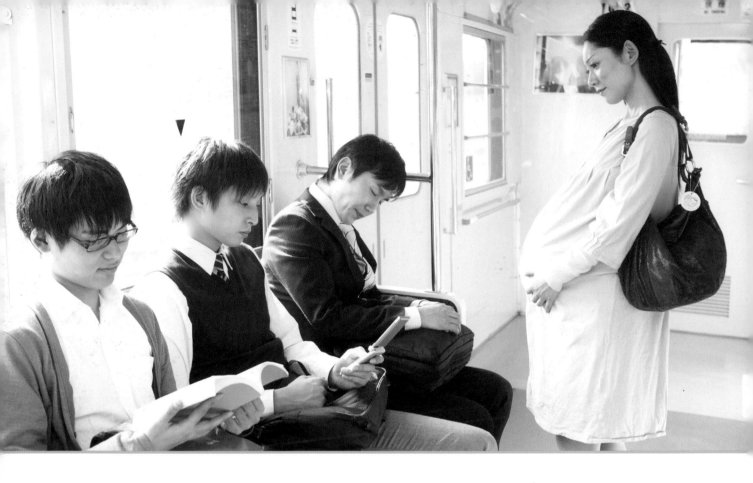

Don't sit down if someone needs a seat more than you.

Ask if they would like your seat.

Don't push in front of people.

Wait your turn.

Don't pick your nose.

Use a tissue to wipe your nose.

Special places

It is important to talk quietly in some places.

It is important not to touch things in some places.

Everywhere you go

litter

Never drop litter. Litter spoils places for everyone.

Put litter in a bin.

Don't put your feet on seats.
It will make them dirty for everyone.

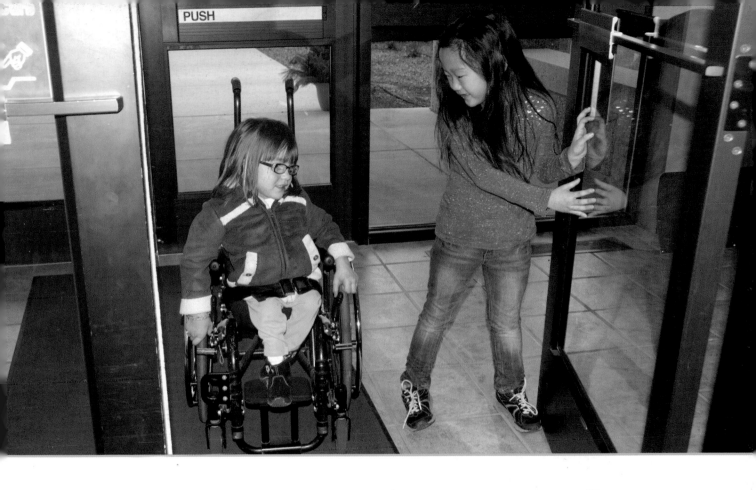

Hold doors open for other people.

Treat people the way you want to
be treated.

People with good manners make the world a nicer place to be.

Best behaviour

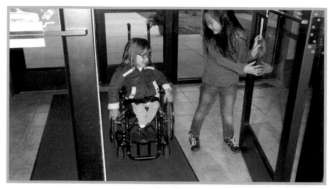

Which person here has good manners?

Answer on page 24

Picture glossary

good manners ways of behaving politely and well

litter rubbish

Index

> **Answer to question on page 22**
> The girl holding the door open for someone
> has good manners.

Notes for parents and teachers

Before reading

Explain that good manners are ways of behaving – they help us to understand what to do and how to act. They are important because they show us how to treat each other and help us to get on well with other people. What examples of good manners can the children think of? List these together.

After reading

- Ask the children to share examples of good manners and bad manners they've seen when they have been out to different places. For any examples of bad manners, discuss together what that person should have done.
- Tell the children to imagine they are organizing a school trip (this could be for younger pupils). Divide the children into groups and ask each group to decide where they will go. Ask them to think about how the children they take will need to behave. Each group can decide what good manners tips they would give to the children on the trip.
- Give pairs or groups of children examples of good manners when out and about to role-play. Different groups can try this at the same time or groups could take turns and be given more support. Children can guess what is being shown and think about how the people in the role play would feel.